T0113523

The Battle

Making Peace Beyond Words

William McRae

authorHOUSE

AuthorHouse™
1663 Liberty Drive
Bloomington, IN 47403
www.authorhouse.com
Phone: 833-262-8899

Published by AuthorHouse 08/20/2020

ISBN: 978-1-7283-7004-0 (sc)
ISBN: 978-1-7283-7003-3 (e)

Print information available on the last page.

Any people depicted in stock imagery provided by Getty Images are
models, and such images are being used for illustrative purposes only.
Certain stock imagery © Getty Images.

This book is printed on acid-free paper.

Scripture quotations marked KJV are from the Holy Bible,
King James Version (Authorized Version). First published
in 1611. Quoted from the KJV Classic Reference Bible,
Copyright © 1983 by The Zondervan Corporation.

Contents

Preface

As I ponder what to write for this preface, my mind keeps wandering to a peach tree my parents tried to grow when I was a kid. I remember the day they planted the sapling. We had to tie a rope to its trunk to keep it upright. It was only a couple of feet tall when we planted it.

What I remember most vividly about that moment in time was that my mom told me that it would take several years before the tree could produce fruit for us to eat. I could not imagine having to wait years for something to grow strong enough to bear fruit. Being a young child, I wondered what the point was in putting in all this effort for something I could not enjoy now.

Imagine my surprise at the fact that during the next fruit season there were small peaches on the tree. I expected them to grow into full-grown peaches, but of course, they did not. The peaches that grew that season were barely larger than the seed, and I imagine that the taste would have left much to be desired.

Unfortunately, I was never able to eat any peaches from that tree. I do not remember exactly what happened, but that tree was cut down before it grew large enough to bear good fruit.

I have known William McRae since a time when we were both young men in our twenties. After reading this book, I thank God that unlike that little peach tree, I have had the patience to watch William grow and bear fruit that is a blessing to all those who are willing to partake in it.

I am glad that by the grace of God, he was able to overcome the battles mentioned in this book. I pray that the hard-earned wisdom that he shares will be as much of a blessing to you as it has been to me.

Read and observe the heart of a man of God who is willing to be transparent with us. I know the character of this man and can testify that he is not just a man of words. He is a doer. I have seen the fruit in his life over many seasons and now you will get to see it as well.

-Timothy Thorpe

Introduction

If you struggle in the areas of Identity, Depression, Fatherhood, Family, Faith, or Fear, then I am here to tell you this is the book to read. I will cover the areas of my struggles and what causes me to gain strength and courage to change my circumstances. I will share how you should never give up or quit on yourself. I was raised in a dysfunctional family, but I never let that hold me back. I always persevered through my problems and sought outside help in my areas of need.

When you begin to read this book, you will see that I touched on a lot of layers that people face daily. Whether it is big or small, no matter what happens in life, always remember God is the best thing for your life.

> "But seek ye first the kingdom of God, and his righteousness; and all these things shall be added unto you." (Matthew 6:33 KJV)

Chapter 1

Identity

"An identity would seem to be arrived at by the way in which the person faces and uses his experience."

-James Baldwin

The question I ask myself is who are you? First, I am a Man of God. Second, I am a Husband. Third, I am a Father. Lastly, I am a family man.

My Feelings

Sometimes in this world, you can get lost in social society. If you are not careful you find yourself simply going with the flow. Fortunately for me, I have never been a follower. I have always been a leader in everything I do. Being a leader comes with both great sacrifice and gratitude when dealing with people. I have been blessed to be a leader in school, church, home, and business.

Facing Challenges

What I learned over the years is that running a business is a challenge on a lot of levels. You must give a lot of yourself to the people you serve for your business to grow successfully. My advice on serving is to make sure people are happy and have what they need. You will keep them coming back by showing good customer service and being very knowledgeable about the business and my community. People will tend to build trust with you and continue to spread the positive word about the business.

Service

The best advertisement is word of mouth. It can help you or hurt your service level.

Man of God

Being labeled a Christian is one of the hardest walks in life. What I mean by that is when people see God's blessing on your life, some people will follow you, and some people will try to crucify you because of disbelief and lack of knowledge.

Challenges

Everybody has an opinion. Some like to challenge your faith with other religions, and some like to test you (women). They try to put you in situations that can be complicated. I just block them out by keeping my eyes on the Lord and what He promises me for my obedience to Him. The only way the devil gets power is if you give it to him. You must constantly stay focused.

Chapter 2

Trust

"Few things can help an individual more than to place responsibility on him, and to let him know that you trust him."

                                    -Booker T. Washington

"Trust" is defined as confidence faith or hope in someone or something

Being true to yourself is one of the best gifts we can pass on to others and the people we love. In my opinion, trust starts with honoring a person and the love they have for you. Trust is always earned and not given to you.

I was about 8 years old before I learned what trust really means. I learned earlier that you can hold people accountable for what they say and do. When someone tells me, they are going to do something, I always believed their word until I see otherwise.

Sometimes my family may try to forget what they told me, but I always quickly reminded them of what they said. As you can see understanding trust started for me at a very young age

Heart - Is a muscular organ in humans that pumps blood through the blood vessels of the circulatory system. Blood provides oxygen and nutrients as well as assisting the removal of metabolic wastes.

An example of the heart is what you listen to when You make decisions based out of love.

The person's heart always tells you about

their character. About my relationship with my mom, I could never understand how a mother could leave her kids to just have fun and party with her friends. My brother and I always asked the question to each other, "How would things be if the table was turned, and mom was not living in the fast lane?"

I think for me it would have made me a better man inside and out. It would have made me look at life from a different view, and I would have made better choices for myself.

When I think about my heart, I can feel the pain of others and feel the weight they carry. To me, a person's heart should be filled with joy, peace, and happiness. I remember a saying that to be happy you must be around happy people.

When I matured, I began to understand what it means to be happy. It helped that I began to apply the Word of God to my life. I instantly felt the change and my attitude started changing. My words were different, and the people started noticing my character was maturing.

In my opinion, your heart is the most important part of your body because it is the central part that controls the flow through your body. What people do not understand is if you have a bad heart then your days are numbered, but with a good heart God will restore your years with grace and mercy.

When I am playing with my dog I always wonder if he can detect what I am feeling on the inside, and the answer is yes. There is something amazing about animals as opposed to humans. A person cannot fake if they are a good person or not to animals, but humans can be fooled for a while until you get caught. If I had to choose, I would rather have the gift of an animal because it protects you from bad-hearted people. When I am around my dog, I always try to have positive energy because it puts him in a good mood.

It is true what they say that a dog is a man's best friend. When the world hates you, your dog always loves you. King Caesar is my dog's name.

My advice to people is if you have a bad heart seek help and pray that God can change your situation. If you have a good heart my advice to you is to keep doing what you're doing and keep surrounding yourself with positive and progressive people that enjoy a spiritual and natural way of living.

Giving Heart

Over the years I learned that giving and receiving is another form of a connection between two people. That is until we learn to give from the heart like Christ when we receive the ultimate gift from Christ, salvation grace, and mercy. The journey we are all on is the journey of self-consciousness and the choices that will determine the outcome of our path

Power of Love

Love is the best gift for all mankind. Love also makes people feel safe and secure and worthy. With real love, you spend most of your days happy and joyful.

The heart fills the mouth. What you say to people comes from the inside of you. I had to learn this. I used to cuss like a sailor before I got saved by grace.

When I was little, I remember my childhood friends and I always used to use curse words toward each other. Whether we were fighting, playing sports, chasing girls, or showing off, in my mind, I assumed it was a male thing to do because a lot of the men in the community curse like sailors too. (LOL)

However, when my grandma sat me down, she said the words you speak come from your heart. It took me a while to understand. When I got older, I began to see what she was saying. "She also said be careful what you say because you never know who you're going to offend and once you release the words out of your mouth you can't take them back." Now since I am forty-one, I learned to think before I speak.

The process I think a person performs under pressure comes is:

- First thoughts in mind
- Second heart feelings
- Third words negative or positive
- Fourth actions negative or positive

When a person gets so mad, the level of their anger during that time determines if they follow all the steps. Some people react first then they think about it later which is the reverse. Most people like me think first then react later. The way I feel in my heart is that it's the right way to handle situations. Whether it is positive or negative, you must always take a minute to think and analyze before making decisions

Actions

I was always told, "Do as I say and not what I do." I had always had a problem with this saying because it set the wrong image to younger people that are growing to become an adult.

Being a young kid, I tried a lot of things when I was young like sex, drinking, and smoking pot. I was making bad choices way younger because of my surroundings. This phase in my life didn't last too long once my grandma and her friends found out what I was doing.

I knew once that happened my grandmother was going to kill me because she always thought a lot about me. After all the beatings and the memorable language, it made me a better man and a better person towards life itself.

Chapter 3

Family

"In every conceivable manner, the family is linked to our past, bridge to our future."

-Alex Haley

Being a Father

Being a father is one of the greatest gifts. God allows me to lead my children. I remember the time when my firstborn came into the world. I was so overjoyed and filled with happiness that I was going to be a father. When I first held her, I cried tears of joy and just did not want to let her go. It was an instant bond that could not be broken. As I looked at her, I noticed that she looked just like me. My grandmother said, "Boy, you got some strong genes, or her mother didn't like you too well during pregnancy."

I just laughed and said, "You probably right, but I'll go with strong genes,"

Also, when I look back on my daughter's mom and me, we did not work out, but we managed to be co-parents for our daughter. However, it took many years to get to that place.

Now she is eighteen going on nineteen next month. I always ask myself, "Where did the time go?" The hardest part of being a parent in the teenage years is fighting the little boys off and reminding your child that "I have been where you are and I have traveled to where you are going, so I know from experience how you feel."

So, to all parents, do not give in just to keep your child happy. It is ok to disagree when it comes to the truth of their welfare. Kids also like to play both parents against one another to try to manipulate the rules of your home. My advice is to stay firm but loving at the same time.

Baby girl is the last of the pack. She brings so much joy and happiness to the family, and I truly believe if she was not here, my family would fall apart. She holds the piece to our puzzle that makes it complete. She is the type that can be bossy, loving, kind, emotional, and happy all at the same time. I could not ask for a better child because she has a heart of gold. Everybody that meets her says that she just knows how to bring happiness to people.

With me being a book author, you would think that she would like reading, but she likes to drag along, so I keep motivating her to work hard and be the best she can be. I strive to be a good example of how hard work pays off.

She also came out looking just like me and her sister Khilah. When I first laid eyes on her,

I remembered what my grandmother said to me, "Either you have some strong genes, or you made that woman upset during pregnancy."

I just chuckled in the inside. I must say I am blessed that God gave me another child to make up for the times I missed with the first one. I am now a full-time Dad. I could not ask for anything more.

Journey

Discovering my calling is something that I am still trying to do. First, when you are a hard worker, it is hard to discover who you really are because you are being pulled in a lot of directions, like fatherhood, being a husband, friendships, business, and helping the community, church, etc.

I will be 42 years old next year and looking back from high school to now I have met all my goals except one. The one I have not reached yet is still an ongoing process that I can not discuss at this current time but will conclude in my next book. Now I am at the point in my life where I am making new goals and setting them higher, so I can keep moving forward.

Chapter 4

Fatherhood

"Any fool can have a child. That does not make you a father. It's the courage to raise a child that makes you a father."

-Barack Obama

Fatherhood - Is defined as the state of having one or more children and spending time with them and getting to know them. The word father (Dada or Papa) is the first word a kid says before learning how to speak properly.

Fatherhood Failures

First, I must admit that my shortcomings as a father started when I first became a father. What I am explaining in this passage is that to be a good father you must be taught how to be a father. I was not taught by my father due to his busy work schedule, so it put me in a place to learn as you go and to seek the proper knowledge from outside sources connected to God.

My first child was born on January 22, 2001, and when she came into the world I cried. When I got the news that she was healthy and beautiful my heart was full of joy.

One problem I have about this situation is that her mother kept me away from her for about a week and I did not get to bond with her the first week, but for the next nineteen years, I made sure I was there and a part of her life even while she was living in Georgia and I was here in North Carolina.

Another failing I had been a father was not being married to the mother. I had a price to pay when I decided to have a baby outside the will of God. I was too young to be having a child and I was not fully prepared for what was to come.

After years passed, her mom and I worked out our differences. We started to forgive each other focusing on the baby. When we did this our relationship got better.

As time went on, I also failed as a father by not spending enough time with my daughter due to my work schedule and distance. From North Carolina to Georgia is about 6 hours' drive. At the time I thought I did enough, but I was not doing the best I could do. I decided that if I cannot see her, I will make sure the communication is good and that she is financially stable.

In my mind, I feel I failed because I didn't spend as much time as I wanted to with my first child, so now with my second daughter everything I needed to work on in my first daughter's life is working in my second daughter's life. The reason for this is because we did it God's way. My wife and I waited a year after we were married to decide we were going to have a child. My decision making was not good in the past, but I wanted to make sure I did things the right way in the future.

Now she is about to be nine years old. She is full of love, compassion, and happiness. I could not ask for a better child. She is definitely the center of our family that holds everything together. I thank God every day for giving me a second chance to be a better father.

With a lot of prayer from friends and family, my life as a father is getting better. Every day my presence in the home makes all the difference for my daughter and myself. Again, I thank God for a second chance.

Winning at Fatherhood

The communication with all my children has gotten better over the years and watching them grow into their own personalities and seeing them respond to situations without momma and I being involved is a beautiful thing to see. As a father seeing that your children are growing up and doing what they are supposed to for themselves and not getting into trouble and not running the streets is a great blessing. I thank God for all of them and I thank God for their mothers helping, leading, and teaching while I work and provide for the family. Lastly winning at being a father is not giving presents but being present in your children's life.

Responsibility

As a father, I am commanded to be there for all my children in all circumstances. First, a father must support the children's vision because everyone has their own journey to follow. A father must also lead by example so that the children can see him doing the right thing and giving them a trail to follow. A father must love all his children the same and not show favoritism to one child. You must love them all the same despite their differences and the calling God has for them.

Chapter 5

Fear

"I have learned over the years that when one's mind is made up, this diminishes fear."

—Rosa Parks

Marriage

Fear - Is an unpleasant emotion caused by the belief that someone or something is dangerous. It implies anxiety and usually loss of courage. Fear is also a shock of sudden startling fear.

The fear I have as a husband is not meeting my expectations as a husband and a father.

The first fear I have as a husband is losing my wife from something tragic and having to raise the kids by myself and take on being a single dad.

My second fear is divorce. This fear bothers me so much. All the hard work and time you put in a relationship and your spouse is not meeting their responsibility of keeping their commitment to the marriage. It always can cause things to go from good to bad very fast if they do not put the work in.

Marriage is not a one-sided way of living. It is two people trying to become one and live life together. Marriage is about making good choices together. It can be in finance, spirituality, intimacy, discipline, and respect for each other.

Always remember to do everything in love with God's guidance directing your path.

Fear Family

My fear for my family is not seeing my family live their best life according to God's vision for their life. My second fear is living this life without knowing each other and not spending time as a family living and learning things about each other and supporting one another. My prayer that I give to God is to keep me and my family safe and protect our minds, heart, and vision, so we can be better people and love one another the way He loves us (unconditional love).

Friends Fear

Friend - A person who accepts you for who you are. They cherish time together and each other's feelings and love you no matter what.

My fear for my friends is them not being there for me when I am at my lowest point or my highest point in life. A friend to me is someone who accepts you and trusts you for who you are and does not judge you for your wrong or right decisions.

A lot of times I look back and I ask myself why I never had the important things in my life that I needed to make life whole. First, I always wanted my family to be like the Cosby's and everybody coming together. I have not had that experience yet to this day.

At forty-one years old I have gone through all my life without experiencing what having a true friend is like. Trying to navigate through life by myself can also turn into loneliness and depression which I struggled with for years, but I always ask God to protect me and continue loving and caring for me.

Despite my situation, through God's grace and mercy, he will make all things right for your good. To survive I always keep that in my mind and heart. In dealing with this dark side in my life God always kept my heart soft and not bitter. That is where my caring and giving to others really developed from.

What I am saying is that what I have someone else will also have. Even if my life is not complete, I love to see other people's lives being complete. My main drive is to encourage and motivate others.

One day a person that comes to my business on a regular basis asked me, "What do you want to do for the rest of your life?" I was caught off guard at first because I am always the one asking people what their goals are. It is not common that people ask me questions like that because they think my life is complete. It may be from the outside, but my inside is still under construction which they can't see.

My answer to his question is I want to serve God, serve people, and preach the gospel to millions of people across the world, and most of all help Down syndrome people, deaf people, and homeless people by making the world a better place for all people. It took me a while to figure out what my purpose is in connection to people but now I know the answer (keep serving).

Business Fear

Business - Is a person's regular occupation profession or trade; a place where people work to make and sell products or services. A business owner is a person who hires people; from work, it earns a profit

My fear for my business is not being able to meet my expectations and giving people the best customer service and the best experience with my business. What I do is leave it all to God and let Him direct my path, renew my mind, and take total control of my life. If you follow these steps you will never have to worry or feel fearful ever again.

Ever since I have been in business, I can honestly say I have not had a downside in my business. Since I started in Graham, North Carolina, my business has always been a success because I totally surrender to God and stay obedient to my assignment (calling) in my business.

Now 14 years later God keeps me going and gives me the strength to be able to help others. He allows Me to make my place of business a safe haven for the lost and for the found. When people come to the shop it reminds me of the church, the place where people can get resources and fellowship, be a part of the community, and give back to those in need (the distribution center).

Chapter 6

Depression

"I don't think that we are a species or a people that can exist without making mistakes somewhere along the line."

-Harry Belafonte

Depression – means loss of sleep, physical changes, sickness, bad attitude, loss of energy, lack of social interaction, and creating bad habits.

In this chapter, I am opening myself up for the healing and support of others that struggle with depression.

Depression first started for me when I was a little boy wondering when my Mom and Dad were going to give me the love I deserve. I cried many nights when my mom was telling me she was coming to pick me up. I would have my bag packed and ready to go, but she never came. She always made excuses for her actions, but that still was not good enough. That happened so regularly that made me numb. I found it hard to trust and I guarded my heart. Out of forty-one years, I can count on both hands how much time we spent together.

About three years ago, I sat down with her in Siler City at a café just to get some closure on the things that took place in our lives. I must say I was relieved, sad, happy, and heartfelt all at once. I had to know, "Why?" and "How it happened?" and "What happened?", so she agreed to talk about the events I went through with her. I heard a lot within those two hours that made me love my mom even more.

Whether she knows it or not she is the centerpiece in my marriage. How I treat my wife is based on my mother. Moms are always a boy's first love, so that is why I needed closure so I can be a better man, father, and husband.

My father, he was always my hero and still is until this day. My dad was a hard worker, but he also had a lot of street smarts. I think his struggle was balancing between good and bad.

I must say he was a good provider, but he struggled with being supportive when it comes to me playing sports or emotionally. It affected me and caused my desire for playing sports to go down because my dad had to work a lot and never had time to be there. On the other hand, I think my work ethic comes from him, however, spending time with my kids made me a better father. I refuse to repeat the cycle of being absent in my kids' life.

Depression started with issues with both of my parents, and it continued through the years in dealing with other relationships with family members. I was always the type of person that took care of business and did things my way, but I handle all my imperfections differently. I have always been a loner and wanted true friends but always get disappointed when I allow myself to get close to someone.

In dealing with my experiences with people, I noticed that when you get close to people, they tend to run away, but when you keep your distance people tend to be more welcoming (confusion). I never understood that behavior because when I love, I love hard. When I am a friend, I am loyal. In the world we live in today, people struggle with both and everybody keeps to themselves rather than speaking and loving one another.

When people see me, they think, I have it all figured out, but they do not know that I struggle with depression, loneliness, and fear. I am human just like everybody else, but I also gain strength in my pain and struggles. The only way I move forward is by God's grace and mercy which he bestowed upon my life.

My early childhood, not having my mom and dad's support, loss of old friends, relationships ending, and people that I hurt in my life is what causes depression to be a struggle for me. Each day through prayer, God's grace and mercy always help me to get better with my emotions, thoughts, and communication.

"Being true to yourself" is one of the best gifts we can pass on to others and the people we love.

Chapter 7

Loneliness

"One and God make a majority.
                    -Frederick Douglass

Loneliness - Sadness because one has no friends or company, "feelings of depression and loneliness":

As a little boy, I discovered that I was different from the other kids in my community. I was an imaginative thinker and I always looked deeper than my friends when it came to analyzing situations.

I remember telling my grandmother one day that my friends and I were about to do something stupid. I also told my grandmother that would not do what my friends asked me to do because it did not make sense to me. However, my friends went ahead and did it. It was a stupid mistake, and they got in trouble. My friends told me I was a scaredy-cat and I laughed and said, "When you all get in trouble, I'll be outside laughing at you while I am with other friends." (LOL)

I knew then that I was not a follower but a leader for doing what is right. Being a leader puts you in a place of loneliness because the number of people in your circle of friends begins to decline because you are different.

Isolation is another form of loneliness

because you separate yourself from people, places, and things. If you are not careful you can easily disconnect yourself from the world. A lot of days I isolate myself from people because I feel we do not have a lot in common whether it is communication or physical activities. Seventy percent of me goes into my work, twenty percent into my family, and ten percent into friends, traveling, and social events. With my crazy schedule, I isolate myself when I have free time, just so I can have peace of mind and enjoy my relationship with God.

Pros and Cons of Isolation

Pros 1st – Spiritual Connection means creating a quiet place so you can hear the Lord without worldly distractions or interruptions even your loved ones. Creating these types of environments helps the interior of your spirit so you can remain strong in your faith walk with the Lord.

Key Point – Spend at least fifteen minutes a day with God.

Pros 2nd – Defying yourself helps you know who you are, where you come from, and where you want to go. When you discover who you are, everything else in your life has purpose and meaning. Remember isolation can be good at times to help you discern who you are so you can be your best self.

Cons 1st – Stress causes one to isolate themselves from a normal environment due to pain, loss of a loved one, relationships, job, or abuse.

Cons 2nd – Isolation can be a symptom of depression which causes your mood to change and your attitude to become negative. A person who is persistently in a bad mood, experiences a limited pleasure, and has no interest in daily life, can become hard to motivate, but through prayer and thanksgiving, God will renew your mind and give you a burst of strength that you need to make it through the day.

"Self Image" is a development that determines the way you think and speak. If you need help do not be scared to let someone know because you are not alone, and other people's stories can be like yours if not worse. Keep your head up and continue to look up and always give God the glory.

Friends

In life, I can count on one hand the number of true friends that I have in my life today. If I think hard about it, I probably started out with two hands worth of friends or what I thought were friends. A true friend is someone who supports you one hundred percent no matter what. A friend is honest with you whether it is something good or bad. A friend is someone who knows you better than yourself. My friend circle has always been small due to trust issues that I have dealt with since my childhood.

I look at friendship as having your friend's back one hundred percent, but I always felt that I did not receive that same bond in return when different situations came up. All the friends that I grew up with do not even hang out or come to each other's houses for social gatherings. The only place I might see someone is at Walmart in passing. When I see them, it is like meeting a stranger due to physical changes and life changes. I never thought that life would turn out like this.

I remember back in the day a place called Morgantown where I grew up used to be the place to be for Black folks. It was truly a community that supported each other. The adults in that community had permission to whip you before your parents got to you. It was hard back in those days because everything we did our parents always knew before we got home.

When I was a young boy, I was hard-headed. I liked to test the water until I would get in trouble then I would sit down when I saw my grandmother get upset. She would knock me upside my head until I got my senses back. I would not trade anything for that experience because people enjoyed each other and their community.

Now that time has passed on into my adult life, I look at the world (friends) in two different ways. First, a "Business friend" is someone you share your life with through work or to whom you provide a service with your work. This kind of relationship exists for a limited time. When the work is over for that day or week, the communication stops. Also, this type of friendship depends on how long you have been working on your job. The friendship also depends on how much you are willing to give of yourself or trust someone. Communication can be categorized as work-related because most of your communication involves work and is meant to help accomplish the task you must do for that day with your coworker or work buddy.

I must say for me work has become my main priority outside of my family. I have made so many friends with my line of work. My work has become personal which I did not expect it to be like that, but what God has for you is for you. Usually, most people separate business from personal.

Secondly, a "Personal friend" is someone you confide in with honesty, trust, laughter, love, and respect. This type of friend knows you inside and out and always has your best interest at heart just like it is their own. Accountability is always there. You can trust that they can keep all information confidential. Laughter is abundant in these friendships along with happiness. Love is always unconditional and pure.

In my life today, I have 3 to 4 people that I call true friends. These guys are good men, husbands, and fathers. I can say again that if I need anything these guys will come to my rescue with no hesitation and will be there for me any time of the day. Lastly, these guys have a relationship with God, and they don't mind sharing the gospel with me. Our friendship gives me an opportunity to have a corporate fellowship with God's word to help me become a better man.

Wife – is a companion, mate to her husband or partner who is considered a helper to her mate and an aid to his vision that is given by God.

When my wife and I met my life was somewhat of a mess. At the time I was running from woman to woman trying to find love in the wrong places and causing a trail of pain for myself and the women I was dating at that time. My grandmother always told me, "Hurt people hurt people." until you face your fears or the truth of the problem.

My issues all originated with my relationship with my mother. I did not understand why the choices I made and the people I hurt all stemmed from my mother until I got in my late twenties. By that time, I was mature enough to figure out what the problem was.

It took having a relationship with God and totally surrendering to Him before I could change my ways. I had to become a good man for myself first and then begin to prepare myself to be a good husband.

As time went on, I thought my time was running out on finding a good one for me, but God said, "When you are at your worst, I still see your best." God never gives up on me and he always keeps me covered and protected because he knows the calling I have on my life.

Beautiful

One day a lady came to my Barbershop to get her son a haircut. She was plain Jane, but she did not have to dress up to get my attention. Her smile could light a room up. That is when I knew something was special and different about her.

Other women were coming to my place of business trying to impress me with the outside appearance, but I was already used to that. It became normal for me. Because the insides would not connect, I never pursued anything with these women.

My wife to be, impressed me with her simple bib overalls on and that beautiful smile. It was totally different from what I was used to.

Time went on and we talked about the possibility of us being more than friends after she took care of her situation she was dealing with. Before we could be an item, we kept the communication going. It was a connection that I needed.

When she showed me her character and her hard work and dedication, I got nervous. I said to myself, "This woman is serious, and she is not playing any games." Most men run when they see the seriousness of a woman, so I tried to run away many times. I remember an old friend of mine told me that when you find one you will know it and also he said: "You can try to run with no shoes but your life won't get better until you let her help you put them on so you can run together." Amen, Amen, and Amen.

I could not shake this woman, so I told her

you got to be the craziest woman I ever met. I got focused and took her seriously. One year later I proposed to her on two knees not one just to let her know how much I appreciated and loved her unconditionally. Looking back to 10 years ago I still laugh and remember what my friend said, "You can't run with no shoe until you let her help you put them on so you can run together."

Marriage - God's legal and formally recognized union of two people as partners in a personal relationship between a man and a woman.

Older married couples always tell me that to have a successful marriage you must take the good with the bad and to keep working at it. I always took what was said to me and applied it in my relationship.

The way we started in our marriage was not God's way. From the beginning, we both made a lot of mistakes that we are not proud of, but thanks to God's grace and mercy He keeps both of us covered. God's word speaks of reaping what you sow.

During 10 years of marriage, it has been hard

for both of us to agree on the same things in life. There are a few points that we struggle with. One is communication. Two is trust. Three is decisions. Four is finances. Five is discipline the children.

Remember I said earlier God's grace and mercy kept me through the horrible times. Some of our struggles were about stuff others said that causes division among us. The two of us to struggle with the things married couples should be good or solid at.

I tried to make things right between us and it seemed that the devil always knocked us back 2 steps. In my opinion, I felt that I was the one that was fighting the hardest to make sure we continue the journey together.

It gets hard when you feel like the only one pushing to make it work. You start filling that you are alone, and the loneliness begins to set in. It starts making you feel that you are doing it all by yourself.

For years I struggled with this frustration and it caused me not to trust people as much as I should have in certain situations. This feeling of isolation didn't just start between me and my wife. It stems from my mother not being there for me when I needed her the most. It causes me to put my actions into a leadership role faster than I should have with my wife. Growing up too fast can affect you in a lot of ways when you get older because it puts you in a place where you feel you missed out on childhood things or just being a kid.

As a kid transitioning into a young man, I grew up very fast and struggled hard emotionally. Some days I felt like I am going through the same thing my mother put me through with my spouse by not being there emotionally. However, I trust God will turn things around for us this year in 2020 which makes 10 years January 2nd

Family - A group of people related to one another by blood or marriage.

When my grandmother left this side of the world, she left a huge hole in my heart. There were so many questions that haven't been answered about my past that she would never talk about. It was a very painful situation when she passed away. It felt like she was always the centerpiece to the family. She held all the information about my family. Her death put me in a place of loneliness, depression, frustration, and isolation, but again God always sends in the right people when you least expect it.

Father

There are some who do not live by the title of father. They are just being a sperm donor. My father is a man who is willing to step up and take care of his children and his family. Anyone can be a father, but it takes someone special to be a dad.

In my situation, I have a great father that was good for financial support, street smarts, entertainment, and strength. However, what I needed from my father the most was the communication, advice, love, spiritual guidance, and knowledge about how to be a good father and husband. These things I had to seek outside due to lack of understanding on my father's part.

In the craziest way, my father is still my hero and love him no less due to his shortcomings as a father. I thank God every day for him being my father and being my friend. Now our relationship gets better every day because we learn a lot about each other. We respect each other as men.

My life is good and blessed for having both parents still living. They both have good health and strength for their age.

Positive Points

Positive experience helps you be a positive person

Knowing that you can remember the positive memories can help you be a good person

Instead of focusing on a negative focus more on positive experiences

Chapter 8

Forgiveness

"True forgiveness is when you can say, "Thank you for that experience"

-Oprah Winfrey

Forgiveness - Is a conscious deliberate decision to release feelings of resentment or vengeance towards a person or group who harmed you regardless of whether they actually deserve your forgiveness.

What the Bible says about forgiveness is "Be kind to one another." (Numbers 14:18) and "The Lord is slow to anger abounding in steadfast love, but He will by no means clear the guilty." (Luke 6:37) "Judge not and you will not be judged forgive not you will not be forgiven."

What the Bible says about forgiveness is "To be kind to one another teaching each other forgiving one another as God in Christ forgave you." That is the good news. Do not forget that we receive forgiveness and in turn, you should be kind and forgiving to those around us. The Lord has forgiven you so you also must forgive.

Family Forgiveness

When I look back over my life my relationship with my family on both sides needs improvement. First, communication was not something we were good at, and expressing how you feel was not in the cards except when anger comes. The only way my family came together was when somebody needs something like money or during the death of a family member. I know that people are busy working and taking care of their business. However, there is no excuse for all of us not to make time and to support one another together as a family.

My prayer for my family is to spend more time together. Most of all we need to communicate how we feel in love, not when somebody makes you mad or upset. I also want our family to know each other and our kids to know each other because one day they will grow up and become adults and try to start dating. The last thing I want is one of my kin trying to date my children without them knowing they are somehow related.

I always had a dream to buy a house with a lot of land in the country and have all my family gathered together to eat and fellowship outdoors on a long wooden handmade table in the middle of the yard, kids playing and running and having fun (the good life).

My forgiveness for my family comes from forgiving myself first. First, I forgive myself for not putting all my effort into the family coming together. Second, I forgive my parents for not being able to help me in the areas that I struggled with when I was young. Third, I forgive my grandmother for not leaving a legacy for the family to follow and not making sure the family stayed close together. Lastly, the McRae and Robinsons family, which I forgive for not having that relationship, communication, and spiritual and physical support. I pray a lot for my family. Even if I do not get to see them, I always keep them in our family prayer.

Wife Forgiveness

When two people come together, they both bring good and bad behavior to the relationship. Past and present behavior has an impact, but what each of us must do is to focus on the positive and not the negative for us to succeed as a couple.

In this chapter of forgiveness, my emotions got the best of me. It was a challenge for me to be able to share my feelings and emotions about my 10 years of marriage. In the first year, it was a challenge for me to adjust and understand what to do and how to share life with my partner in God's way. My parents were not successful in having a healthy marriage for me to follow which made it more challenging for me.

I have always been the type of person to take care of things immediately and not have to wait for someone else's approval to do what's right. My wife is the type of lady that likes to wait and exhaust all her options before fixing any problem. I am the opposite. Whenever something comes up, I deal with it right then and not sit back and wait for somebody else to do it. It was hard for me in the first years of marriage having to adjust to someone so different from me in a lot of areas.

Faith without works is dead, but with the help of God, it did get easier to handle situations and problems differently. Patience is something I had to learn very fast in order to keep my marriage successful. When people ask me questions about marriage, I always start off by asking, "Do you all have a foundation?", meaning is God in the center of your relationship. Secondly, "How well do you know each other's family?", so you can have a better understanding of each other's backgrounds. Knowing each other's strengths and weaknesses is important. Thirdly, "Do you trust each other one hundred percent in basic areas of marriage: spiritual, communication, finances, respect, faith, and sex?" The couple's answers always determine if the couple is ready for marriage.

My forgiveness toward my wife was hindered by not being able to understand our differences and the struggles we've been through in a timely manner. When I began to accept her for who she is I knew then that God is really working on my heart and mind so that I can be the best husband I can be and the father of our children. Finally, I think the most important thing I learned in my marriage is that you cannot change the past, but you can control your future.

Friends Forgiveness

True Friend - Is someone who has your back when things are going wrong or when they are going right. A friend is also someone who does not lead you or follow you. Instead, they walk with you.

Most of my true friends came along in my later years, and my associates are people I deal with every so often. One thing I can say in life is that you can have a lot of things but there is nothing that can compare to a true friend.

My forgiveness to all my friends involves not spending enough time with each other or hanging out outside our busy schedules. I blame myself first for not fitting in enough time despite my super busy schedule. When I step back and look at what I do, I make my own schedule. I own several businesses and determine how things go from day to day. In my wife's words "If you can make time for other stuff you can make time for your friends." I had to accept that she is right about that.

I don't know everything that my friends have going on, but I hope and pray that soon we can have a long friendship together and celebrate each other's family when we come together. Whether it is good times or bad times, I believe and trust that everything will come together in God's time.

Chapter 9

Social Life

"Associate yourself with people of good quality, for it is better to be alone than in bad company."

-Booker T Washington

Social Life- The part of a person's time spent doing enjoyable things with others.

I enjoy traveling to gain knowledge. By seeing other cultures and religions that are not your norm it will broaden your horizons.

First, the activities that I enjoy are golf, running, riding motorcycles and ATV's, and traveling with friends and family.

Golf is my relief break from all the hard work I've done weeks before. It is kind of like a treat for yourself.

Running is my therapy. It helps me relax, keeps me energized and healthy. Running also helps me relieve stress and helps me increase my relationship with God when I run. Running helps me clear out the mind. It helps the healing in the body.

The motorcycle is my adrenaline rush when I have a need for speed or just having fun with friends and family.

Happiness - is the feeling that comes over you when you know life is good and you cannot stop smiling. It is the opposite of sadness. Happiness is a sense of well-being, joy, or contentment. When people are successful, they feel more secure.

Happiness for me is traveling across the world learning different cultures and meeting new people (student mode). I enjoy trying different foods. Sometimes I just like being home with family watching movies or playing with my dog King Caesar.

Chapter 10

Freedom

"You can't separate peace from freedom because no one can be at peace unless he has his freedom."

-Malcolm X

Freedom - the power or right to act speak or think at once without hindrances or restraint; the state of not being imprisoned or enslaved.

My freedom is being able to be what I want when I want to do it. That is what an entrepreneur is to me. Working for yourself and your family without someone controlling your time and your life makes you free from bondage.

Freedom is not free. It comes with sacrifice, time, commitment, and dedication. If you can follow these principles your business will be successful. Always put God first in everything you do because without him being involved you cannot do anything. Hard work pays off.

Author Interview

Interviewer: First question, Just a little softball question. The title is <u>The Battle</u>. What's "the battle"? Why did you pick the title and what does it mean to you?

Author: I would say the Lord actually gave

that title to me because I was fumbling around trying to figure out what title to go with.

It just seemed like that one was just more fitting for my story. In life, you are going to go through some ups and downs, and it is all about how you overcome that.

Interviewer: So, did you have anything else you want to say about that?

Author: <u>The Battle: Making Peace Beyond Words</u> and in the story, they will find out why I will put making peace beyond words because your actions must go into play with what you are saying. So, I just feel this is the right topic for that.

Interviewer: Now, this was about 2016 the last book or 2018 was the last book. So, … what do you think has changed in your life since the last book came out.

Author: I see … the growth of me becoming a man, the growth for being a better person, overall better father husband and just a better family member, you know, as far as just being supportive of my family, distant family, just being more active in those areas. And just my spiritual journey has gotten better also.

So, I feel like I'm at a good place man just growing and I'm learning as I go. So, I always keep my mind into a student mentality. So, each situation is different, but I learned from them and try to make some positive about it.

Author: So, let's go back to the first and we're going to like sort of try and trace through the steps.

Your first book was <u>Faith That Kept Me</u>. That book was like it is going through your life. So where was your mind or what would you think was the major thing that the Lord was trying to get you to say in that book?

Author: I think my first book was more just putting my story out there and getting healing through the process. As I released my story to the world and just as I am writing, God is still continuously working on me. So, I can get better in the area that you saw that I was weak in that book and things with my family that we struggled with, and how we came up poor. Just by me telling my story that is going to be an inspiration for some other young man or older man because anybody can relate to any of my books.

Interviewer: The second one was <u>Miracle in You</u>.

Author: All right and that was about the spiritual journey and getting in touch with your spiritual self.

Interviewer: You want to elaborate on that?

Author: I think that was just the area I was at that time. I am still on that journey. There's a continuation … but I was at a good place spiritually and just learning and just discerning more things that I need to be aware of … wisdom just comes with the discernment and spiritual side of it, just instructions from God, they were just directing my steps on what I need to do. Just be a better person.

Interviewer: And the next one was <u>The Journey</u>.

Author: Yes sir.

Interviewer: So, what would you like to say about that.

Author: Oh man I think that's a combination of books one and two and just kind of where I was at that current time. When I was writing that story … just tying it all together and just letting the world know the process.

It's like I have arrived on a lot of levels, but

I never forget where I come from through the process, it's a process you have to go through to get to where you're trying to get to and I just felt like that topic was very fitting at that time of my life, just sharing that and hoping somebody can get inspired by the story.

Interviewer: So now we are up to <u>The Battle</u> and what do you think makes that different from the other three books or … maybe how it is like a sequel to the other books?

Author: Yeah, I think …it is my maturity level now and growth, and becoming a more responsible adult, and becoming a better person.

I was young. 30-year-old man when I wrote the first book. The second book, I was still like in my mid-thirties, then the third was … kind of at the end of my 30s. I'm in my 40s so everything is different now so you just had a different place but it's at a good maturity place, and I'm getting at a really good place to where we at even with my marriage.

I feel like we have been through a lot and we still growing, but we not giving up we are committed to the cause. We have got to be there for the kids and be good road models. I share all that stuff man and I am in a good place.

I think this book is going to be the best one so far because I am opening up more than the other ones. I kind of give you a little bit at a time, but this one I am kind of putting it out there more, and just hoping God just take me to another level. When I do another book, it's going to be something great too.

Interviewer: Now I did notice that you did open up more not that you didn't open up because of course like your first book was basically like it was almost like an autobiography, and of course you revealed a lot in other two books as well, but I felt like in this one you touched on some areas that like, maybe men in general but I know especially like black men or even like let's just say people, human beings, … really don't like to admit like areas in which they've struggled or weaknesses. What made you feel comfortable even discussing those topics?

Author: The maturity level just being able to have the right mindset to get there to share my story and feel comfortable about it, and building my confidence up hearing other people's story or how they share their life story that's a motivation for me to go and just put it out there, and just don't be afraid like they say naked and not afraid, so I mean, you just put your story out there and just see what take place and you can't do anything but heal from it. When you are young and you don't do what you suppose to do; it puts you in a place to have to play catch up, but when you are older you should have the wisdom to navigate.

Interviewer: What do you want people to get out of this book this go-round?

Author: The importance of knowing who you are identifying yourself and being able to stay connected with positivity, and people that are trying to speak wisdom to you. Always listen take the time and learn without getting an attitude like you know everything. We can get caught up in ourselves sometimes.

So, I feel like you got to humble yourself, so humility shows. Like I said connecting with the right people would be a second one.

Interviewer: How did you overcome those challenges or your weaknesses or are you still struggling?

Author: As far as I would say the main ones that I brought up in the book, I pretty much surpassed those areas. That was more of a younger struggle. Once I got older and as you read in the book it's going to tell you that I kind of grew up fast so I had to learn stuff as I go and just kind of work through it and just being around the right people that can tell me the right information.

Just a lot of friends and family praying for me because I need it. ... I challenge anybody if you're feeling weak... talk to somebody, whether it's a therapist, your pastor, or a mentor, or whoever you seek, you need to go see that person just so they can pray or speak with you and help you along your journey.

So, some things that I did to keep me going then was just staying busy working all the time. That was a good way to clear out my head and exercise. I like running so that is a therapy for me, but that is a good time when I can speak to the Lord...and it is just me and Him, and it is some days where I just pulled to the side of the road just to weep. Just to let it out because it can be so much pressure built up. I mean you would be a husband, father you going to go through those struggles... going through stuff, it is only common. We just got to know who to seek to get by. (God)

It was just a growth process for me and just

I need to see both sides in order to figure out which way I'm going to go whether I want to continue to work in corporate or going to figure out my own path, which means owning my own stuff so I chose ownership and I feel like that was the best thing because it opens up a platform for me to help other people, especially young men that look like me. I definitely want to continue that journey because it's a need man.

Yeah like you say you turn the news on what you see young people killing each other, where's the father?

Some kids do not come from good homes.

It takes a lifetime trying to live, right? It can take you a second to lose it all, so that is why you must be conscious and just always surrounding yourself with positive people. That is what works for me.

Continue to protect your eyes or what you are hearing. Read the Word (Bible) daily because that is going to give you that conviction to make you better, to keep your eyes on the truth. I'm at a place where I'm all focused on peace of mind, good health, being there for my children and my wife, and leaving the legacy for them. They are going to be taking care of and I am hoping their kids will be taken care of also.

You must leave something for your children. And I know it is hard sometimes coming from our background. A lot of people in our communities have no fathers in the home, so that should be a motivational factor for all of us that struggle in these areas.

Suggested Bible Reading

"Finally, my brethren, be strong in the Lord, and in the power of his might. Put on the whole armour of God, that ye may be able to stand against the wiles of the devil. For we wrestle not against flesh and blood, but against principalities, against powers, against the rulers of the darkness of this world, against spiritual wickedness in high places. Wherefore take unto you the whole armour of God, that ye may be able to withstand in the evil day, and having done all, to stand. Stand therefore, having your loins girt about with truth, and having on the breastplate of righteousness; And your feet shod with the preparation of the gospel of peace;" (Ephesians 6:10-15 KJV)

"Be ye angry, and sin not: let not the sun go down upon your wrath:" (Ephesians 4:26 KJV)

"And will be a Father unto you, and ye shall be my sons and daughters, saith the Lord Almighty." (2 Corinthians 6:18 KJV)

"Be sober, be vigilant; because your adversary the devil, as a roaring lion, walketh about, seeking whom he may devour: Whom resist stedfast in the faith, knowing that the same afflictions are accomplished in your brethren that are in the world." (1 Peter 5:8-9 KJV)

"Whether therefore ye eat, or drink, or whatsoever ye do, do all to the glory of God." (1 Corinthians 10:31 KJV)

"For though we walk in the flesh, we do not war after the flesh: (For the weapons of our warfare are not carnal, but mighty through God to the pulling down of strong holds;) Casting down imaginations, and every high thing that exalteth itself against the knowledge of God, and bringing into captivity every thought to the obedience of Christ;" (2 Corinthians 10:3-5 KJV)

"For God hath not given us the spirit of fear; but of power, and of love, and of a sound mind." (2 Timothy 1:7 KJV)

"Fear thou not; for I am with thee: be not dismayed; for I am thy God: I will strengthen thee; yea, I will help thee; yea, I will uphold thee with the right hand of my righteousness." (Isaiah 41:10 KJV)

"Why art thou cast down, O my soul? and why art thou disquieted within me? hope in God: for I shall yet praise him, who is the health of my countenance, and my God." (Psalms 43:5 KJV)

"God is our refuge and strength, a very present help in trouble." (Psalms 46:1)

"Let all bitterness, and wrath, and anger, and clamour, and evil speaking, be put away from you, with all malice: And be ye kind one to another, tenderhearted, forgiving one another, even as God for Christ's sake hath forgiven you." (Ephesians 4:31-32 KJV)

"For if ye forgive men their trespasses, your heavenly Father will also forgive you: But if ye forgive not men their trespasses, neither will your Father forgive your trespasses." (Matthew 6:14-15 KJV)

Printed in the United States
By Bookmasters